Jellyfish Dreams

Also by Dianne Kennedy and published by Ginninderra Press
Tea Leaves of the Soul

Dianne Kennedy

Jellyfish Dreams

Sincere thanks to Jera for the gift of her original artwork,
to Naiche for the digital adaptation of it and to Amy
(Ricoh Ulverstyone) for enhancing the image for printing.

Dedicated to Sean and Naiche.
And to Fay Forbes for her friendship, encouragement
and editing skills.

With acknowledgement and sincere thanks also to members
of the Devonport Writers' Workshop for their support and
entertainment.

Some of the poems in this collection have appeared in anthologies
by Ginninderra Press and the Devonport Writers' Workshop.

Jellyfish Dreams
ISBN 978 1 76109 083 7
Copyright © text Dianne Kennedy 2021

First published 2021 by
GINNINDERRA PRESS
PO Box 3461 Port Adelaide 5015
www.ginninderrapress.com.au

Contents

Medusa…
- Medusa — 9
- Her Golden Boy — 13
- Tar-Neem-Er-Ra — 15
- The Last Thylacine at Tulampanga — 16
- The Smallest Apostle — 18
- The Kite — 19

Inundation…
- Inundation — 35
- Dreamcatcher — 37
- A Stitch in Time… — 39
- The final page — 41
- Milkmaid — 43
- Fading to the Future — 44
- Collateral Damage — 46
- The Game — 47

Jellyfish Dreams…
- Jellyfish Dreams — 55
- Painted Desert 1976 — 56
- Mountain Reflections — 57
- Morning Ride Down Oxford Street — 58
- City Lunch Break — 61
- I remember… — 65
- Solace — 67
- Maternal heritage — 68
- Dark Journeys 1942 — 70
- Shards — 72
- Gems of Guilt — 73
- Ancestral Habits — 75

Backyard Adventures	76
We stayed and we played…	78
The Wild Duck	80
Letting Go	81
Mother's Day	82
Tapping	83
Closing Doors at Christmas	85
The Dandelion	87
Wandering Down Memory Lanes	88
Keepsakes	91
The Wreck	92
Roadkill	93
The Ambulance Chaser	95
Seeds of Contentment	97
Dangers of Poetry	100
The Art of Words	102
Stampede	104

Medusa...

Medusa

i

Of the gods' three daughters
only she was mortal,
the one not permitted
to cross the portal
to immortality.
And why did he,
the god of seas,
become enamoured with her
lush golden locks?
His lust surely proof
of her captivating youth.

Did she have a choice,
a voice to say no
or did she willingly go
to Poseidon's embrace?
Envy decided her fate:
the wrath of the warrior goddess.
Athena befouled
her enticing tresses,
changed them to writhing serpents;
worse yet was the curse
on those who caught her eye:
they were turned to stone,
for a ghastly gorgon she was ordained,
reviled, feared and alone.

Her legend grew;
soon she became
a challenging game
to seekers of fame,
until Perseus claimed
the severed prize:
her once noble head
now haloed by vipers,
surrounding her bitter face
with its fatal eyes.

Some say she was a mere metaphor
for victories in ancient war;
when city walls fell
priestess masks dropped
as if, like her,
their heads were lopped.

ii

Eons have passed and through you
her name lives once more.
I watch you disintegrate
on the shore.
White horses roll in
stretching their watery limbs
as if to save you,
but each is drawn back
into the briny depths;
their flowing manes reflect
the magic stallion birthed
from drops of blood spilled:
mighty Pegasus arose
when your mythical
namesake was killed.

Once in captivating
translucent youth
you too pulsated in
Poseidon's realm,
dangling delicate tendrils
as you gave in
to the ocean's whims.
Was it a goddess curse still
that shattered your
strength and your will?
Each tidal propulsion
forced you helplessly
towards land
to dry and die here
on this heartless sand.

Her Golden Boy

At ten years old he surprised his mum
by brushing
his own school shoes.
She shared the news
with her mother, his Nan;
he was acting like a man.
Neither knew
he was hiding a hole
in his left shoe sole.

At twelve years old he surprised his mum
by working,
delivering newspapers each day,
foregoing his time to play.
His mum was proud of her son,
of the young man he'd become
without a dad.
Her lad would earn his own keep;
more peacefully she would sleep.

At fourteen years he surprised his mum
by buying
a new bright red bike;
he rode to the places he liked.
Her words filled with joy
when she spoke of her boy.
Tears she would hide
for she often felt sad
at the poverty they had.

At sixteen years he surprised his mum
by saying
he had a job in the city;
she hid her self-pity
for she understood
it was for his own good.
One last ride
he said he must take
to a spot down by the lake.

He rode out of town
to the place he had found;
knelt on one knee
'neath a gnarled wattle tree;
prayed to the Earth Mother
seeking help for his other.

He came home and surprised his mum
with a branch
of thick yellow bloom,
told her to shake it
in the lounge room.
She smiled and obeyed;
a thick carpet was laid.
He kissed her farewell,
thanked her for her trust.

His gift then turned into
the purest gold dust.

Tar-Neem-Er-Ra

My eyes trace her chiselled face
her rocky façade sculptured by Time
and worn by winds from the west
she rests against the eastern escarpment
her forested skirt flows
into those of two western sisters
shielding sites once sacred to women:
first females chipped ochre here
shared stories   taught lore   birthed new generations
danced and sang the joy   and sadness of living.
From meandering creek   to hidden caves
this land contains memories of
graves of babes born   too delicate to survive;
celebrations   of womanhood attained;
the shared witnessing   of the wisdom of elders.

Newcomers came   altered the cloak of her slopes;
named the lofty trinity: Roland, Claude, Van Dyke.

As I walk the valley track below her peak
treading reverently in awe of her mystery
and secrets held there throughout history
one sorrowful word wafts on the breeze
whispering through branches of ancient trees:
                    Tar-Neem-Er-Ra.

---

* To some of the old people the land to the south of their country, including the mountains, was known as *Tar-Neem-Er-Ra* (big grassy plains).

The Last Thylacine at Tulampanga

Thylacine looked down to the valley
watched the river rolling its silver thread
below grey rocky outcrops jutting
through trees as ancient as time.
He lifted his gaze to the cliffs
thrown up and stacked
with stone masonry precision
by tidal waters eons ago.
Lowering his eyes
he recalled human shadows
scattered along the cave-dotted crest,
chipping and gathering:
for over ten thousand years
the Pallittorre had prized
the rust red, golden and pale ochre therein
to trade with tribes and to adorn their skin.
They would have sensed him there,
but were willing to share their beloved
Tulampanga.

He roamed often, too,
the Mountain of the Spirits:
sacred Kooparoona Niara;
knew its peaks and valleys –
and its refuges,
needed more now that
the shadows had faded,
the caverns deserted,
celebrations silenced.
He alone of old times remained –
though hunted.

The newly arrived called the river Mersey;
the town and nearby rambling creek
they named after the Mole, for water here
through underground caverns would disappear.
The Mountain became the
Great Western Tiers;
Tulampanga, the grey speckled cliffs,
they called Alum.

The Smallest Apostle

Gazing jagged features jutting south;
green life stubbornly dotted upon your dome –
are you watching, waiting, straining to stay
or bearing body forward away from home?
Eons of tidal waters have washed your feet
and once amongst the tallest you stood;
now in prostrated pride you taunt time's decay,
but your leaning pate denotes a desperate mood.
Anchored by the weight of wetted silt,
your death by descent to oblivion is slow
and like other wanderers upon these shores
your defiance denies the presumption you will go.
Your profile dignified by twilight's gold touch
or softened in the purple haze of dawn
reflects bygone spirits of this ancient land
and memories of those who were her first born.

The Kite

According to some versions of the legend of the Egyptian goddess Isis, when her lover Osiris was killed and his body parts scattered, Isis and friends took the form of the kite, the bird of prey, to fetch and restore him. This poem acknowledges the magical powers of the goddess and her descendants as a fictional representation of the myth in modern times.

I

Issi's mama was put in the ground
in an ugly box of wood
pale brown, coldly firm
like the forehead upon which
the child had planted
a farewell kiss.

She will be waiting for you, they said,
in a place called Paradise
beyond the sky.
But she was locked in a box
under the earth…
how could Mama fly?

Issi posed the question
to Papa as he sat slumped,
staring solemnly at the liquid
he poured between thin bitter lips.
Continuing to glare into the glass
he rasped, *Go away, go away!*
unable to share his grief.

Issi's feet dragged her to the shed,
led her to the final gift given and shared
before Mama went to bed
and became dead.

The girl gazed at the feather-patterned
satin-soft material held together
with fine sticks and string:
a wondrous thing
in the shape of the bird
her mama had loved.

Issi tucked it under her arm and
absconded to the cliff-top meadow
through the forbidden gate.
She prayed that her papa might
witness her daring flight:
punishment, though harsh,
would satisfy an aching need
for his touch.

Tears scuttled down her face
as she reached the place alone.
The silence was shattered by
doleful descending shrieks
preceding a piercing *si-si-si-si*.
The mystical bird swooped and swirled
beneath the beckoning sky.

Issi unfurled the fabric,
laid it reverently on the earth:
a mirror image of the kite in flight.
She grasped the handle tight.
Sorrow's drops dried as Issi raised eyes
to the sound of the bird,
heard Mama's lilting laughter
echoing in her ears;
felt her auricles recede and disappear
as a gentle breeze tugged at her toy.
She was aware her hair was hardening
into fine branches sprouting with down.

She skipped over the ground,
her feet becoming light,
legs narrowing with each hopping step.
Her hands melded with the kite's string,
fingers turned to pinions at
the tips of arms, now wings.
Her bones began reshaping,
her body shortening, rounding,
soon enshrouded in feathers the colour
of Papa's drink of forgetfulness.

El Condor Pasa or *If I Could**
was the song her mama had sung
when together, they danced with the kite.

I am… I can!
screeched her soaring daughter,
si-si-si-si!

Triumph shrieked from her beak
as she lifted higher and higher
on her mission
to bring her mama back to earth
       a resurrection,
               a rebirth.

* English lyrics by Paul Simon; traditional Peruvian music by Jorge Milchberg, Essex Music

II

Mama's inspirational kite
joined Issi's metamorphic flight.
Together they soared towards the clouds
till they reached the height
where earthly birds are not allowed
to fly beyond their power.

Banking, Mama's blessed bird
raised wingtips skywards,
pinions pointing west.
Issi, though weary, wheeled higher on this
her now solitary quest.

Tiredness soon engulfed the small girl-bird,
her wings no more retained their rhythm;
each breath like knives at her tiny lungs tore.
Exhausted, she surrendered
to what fate lay in store.

Sighing, she gasped her mama's name
as she began to plummet
back towards earth;
she wondered if they would
ever meet again in some new form,
in Paradise or a place of rebirth.

III

In a realm far beyond mortal dreams
is that ethereal place where godly schemes
some times are entwined with humanity's
perception of its own reality.

Though rare, some mortal beings are blessed
to take a more sacred journey than the rest.

Above the veil between the worlds
the god of light's falcon wings unfurled.
Horus had spied through the astral portal
the frantic flight of one such mortal.

More rapid than human eyes can behold
he broke through the gossamer mist of gold
separating the finite from infinity,
the mortal world and the realm of divinity.

Issi closed her eyes as she tumbled down;
then harkened at a strange whooshing sound;
felt herself raised as powerful claws
clutched her away from death's cruel jaws.

In the talons gripping her bird body tight
Issi felt safe on that fantastic flight.

She slept through the passage of planets and stars,
stirred only when through the barrier they passed
feeling warmth from the delicate threads of mist
which reminded her of her mama's kiss.

Soon she felt herself lowered to the softest bed
and wondered if this was the Paradise of the dead.
Feather gentle hands brushed her cheek
as she sank into slumber, weary and weak.

IV

Issi gasped when she awoke for her feathers had gone;
she felt contented and happy, alive and strong.

Words wove around the baffled child's brain,
reassuring, soothing, and unworldly strange.

A lady sat beside her, bathed in a radiant glow;
with a voice lilting like music, she seemed anxious to know:

Are you our sweet Rosita? Eyes full of hope, she begged
Issi, her body sob-wracked, crumpled back down on the bed,

for the sound of Mama's name sliced her heart and her mind:
she knew it was not here that her mother she would find.

Mama's dead, she stammered, in a grief-stricken moan.
The lady whispered gently, *My child, you'll not be alone.*

Tell how you came here, how did you know?
Issi spoke of the kite toy her mama had loved so.

You have been very brave, now what is your name, dear?
Issi's sorrowful response was washed by her tears.

*Your Mama was wise, that is easy to tell;
she named you for me: Isis… Issi, the same letters spell.*

*Meet your grandfather, Osiris he is called,
and our son, Horus, who stopped your near fatal fall.*

*Tell me, dear Issi, where does your mama lie?
We really must know now 'ere too much time passes by.*

V

Horus and Isis left Issi there, to explore
her new haven safe in the care
of Osiris, god of justice,
who showed her more
of this place, its treasures
and comforts galore.

He poured her some nectar in a
cup of pure gold, then led her onto
the marble balcony to behold
the beauty she would share in eternity;
Issi's mind filled with delight;
her heart with serenity.

Lush gardens spread out as far as
she could see, with creatures and birds
playing in a land of fantasy. She knew that here
she would be safe from all harm,
but she hungered to be held
in Mama's loving arms.

Osiris knew that the child was sad deep inside
and assured her that she must keep hope
alive. He told her the tale of
how he had been saved
after being scattered around
several earthen graves.

He led her down to the garden below; related
their legends that all descendants should know,
of divine ancestry and their land's history; Issi listened
intently to understand the mysteries.
He then told the tragic tale of their loss of her mother
through the callous jealous actions of another.

Back in the palace, they sat to await
the return of their family and to learn Mama's fate.

VI

Five raptors had swooped in a holy glow
through space and clouds to
the earth below.

Isis again had issued a call
to rescue a loved one beyond
the mystical wall.

Earthly kites, too, gathered around
their sacred kin at the site of
freshly dug ground.

To dig was hopeless with claws and wings.
It was Horus who spied
a most useful thing:

a curious hound hovered close by;
the young god approached it,
gazed into its eyes.

The canine responded with an eager bark,
dashed to the grave and
completed the task.

When talons lifted the lid, Isis sighed
in relief that not too much
time had passed by.

Issi's mama lay still in her hard wooden bed.
The mortal birds wept to see
Rosita was dead.

Isis circled three times, then fluttered close,
brushed her beak on Rosita's eyes,
her ears, mouth and nose.

Slowly awakening, Rosita stretched and rose,
smiled as she wriggled
her fingers and toes.

She stepped up, amazed at all the birds' faces;
in wonder she saw the dog
covering all traces

of the miracle that happened under moonlight,
the hound licked her, then quickly
vanished from sight.

Isis explained to Rosita that she was blessed
and thus must come with them now
and leave the rest

of her family; Rosita replied that she'd been found
as a babe wrapped in eastern blankets
in a church ground.

Isis told of the infant stolen by jealous kin
when born to a young goddess who
no longer loved him.

They had searched for her but his magic was strong;
when he fell into darkness
all hope was gone.

Rosita gasped, remembering her own little girl;
she must comfort her daughter before
leaving this world.

Isis held her Rosita close that night,
as she related the tale of
Issi's brave flight.

Farewells were bidden to their earthly bird kind;
in tender talons Rosita was borne
through stars to find

her precious daughter, the heroine child;
joyful tears melded with
their wonder-filled smiles

as they caressed one another, hugged and kissed
in that ethereal place beyond
the golden gossamer mist,

where with sacred kin they reside in eternity
unbound by mortal ideas
of forever's reality.

Inundation…

Inundation

Pulsating forwards
bobbing and weaving
flowing on a tide
of determination,
a current of cause
forcing them on to a
dangerous destination.
Feeding on notions
of freedom and
cultural survival,
a myriad medusae
face the stinging hues
of water bombs.
Yet numbers grow
with each day's
incoming tide
rippling towards
the city centre
to cluster
beneath bridges
or to surge like
an overwhelming
tsunami across walls
of shielded resistance.

Their sole protection:
soft umbrellas,
no defence against
the landing for some
behind bars;
already many bear
battle scars;
their ultimate tragedy
is the inevitability
of all being
fatally beached
by the bullets
of tyranny.

Dreamcatcher

Peace is a broken catcher of dreams
hanging with promises
slowly unravelling through time
being torn to tatters by man
who, some say, began
in a garden of perfection,
who heard he could
become a god and
grasped the fruitful chance.

Ego, envy and greed were to be
his eternal original sin
setting brother against kin;
stones and bare hands
first weapons of small destruction,
supplanted by swords and spears;
people learned how to fear.

Power seekers each year appear
to pattern the planet with death
from canons and guns,
rockets and planes,
while nations' sons seek fame
by killing for a cause,
a country, or a god.

Thus the continuum…

There is no turning around
the inherent nature of man:
there forever will be one
who seeks to command,
inventing insidious ways
to promote his own prestige,
supported by the deeper evil
of those who create and sell
his deadly means.

The frame of the dreamcatcher
erodes more rapidly
with each passing age;
its weaving decays,
it drops in fragments
our dreams of peace
like leaves from a dying tree
in this
the autumnal season of mankind.

A Stitch in Time...

Time tortures idle hours;
persistently pecking at my brain
until it reaches seeds
buried deep in sanity's soil.
A compost of loss
enriches the pain.
Droplets of despair
water bulbs of memory:
a father taken,
a mother spoiled
before slaughter
by black masked men,
and then
two sisters
vanished.
Under darkness of night
I flee.
Finally I catch a boat
which failed to float.
At seventeen
I arrived,
alone, grief stricken,
desperate to be free.
Now planted here
for years numbering three
I wilt in this garden:

sultry, tropical…
enclosed by razor wire;
where blood red blossoms
flourish in barren soil
oozing the poison sap
of taunting hopelessness.
I bleed from the barb…
once, twice,
again and again;
at the final
paired piercing
I tie off the thread.
No more words
must be said
for I have to block
the escape
of the scream
which if allowed
to sound
may never end.

The final page

Flies dapple sunlight already dulled by dust
which powders the discarded dregs of lives.
In the mire of stench and staleness
two glimpses of gold distract:
lion faces glistening amongst debris,
out of place like a zoo escapee,
or a beast labelled rogue for seeking food
too close to human habitat.
These recline on a tattered timber slat.
I glance around… I am alone.
I cross the wasteland as if stepping stones.
A flutter of fragile beige
clings to the drawer I withdraw,
tote back along the mud-caked track
and the security of my car.
Gliding through the unguarded gate
I give a victory smile to the sign:
No scavenging.

Safely in my own domain
I marvel at the beauty of the brass beasts
yet my curiosity elsewhere remains.
Carefully I release the delicate page
the lion knobs guarded over unknown years.
Faded words appear
penned in an English which,
like its writer, is broken…
she by despair.
They tell of her following love
far from her family home;
of her struggle to adapt;
of deep yearning for summer green
and winter forest frosts;
of babes born and lost
to the harshness of this bland land;
of exclusion from neighbours
who never tried to understand
her loneliness and her foreign ways.
In words shakily written, she ends:
I wanted only to find friends,
for my man he is a drover
and he is gone…
he is gone for so long…too long.
No more now for me to do…
        I must go too.

Milkmaid

She with the beautiful eyes,
how she must deeply despise
the family who claims she is theirs
as she stands and vacantly stares.

Is she ruminating on a memory
of a little one's limited longevity
and the brief mother's contentment she knew
for moments numbering too few?

Now bound by mechanical ties
as her bounty is stolen she sighs,
sadly searching from left to right –
no small clone of herself in sight.

Her yearning spirit bleeds
for the loss of her nurturing needs.
What reflects in her gentle brown eyes
are the tears her breaking heart cries.

Fading to the Future

My eyes drift
following the contours
of cleft and ridge
which form the pleated pattern
of the constantly changing hues
of the conglomerate corrugated wall
leading upwards to the
familiar outline delineating
mountain and sky.
Pastures, like thick strokes
from an artist's brush
dabble green against
the blue-grey forested backdrop;
and houses, like staggered
Lego blocks, are scattered
around the base
and haphazardly up
the lower slopes.
My gaze is held by the
Monet daubed foliage of trees:
shelters for eagles, cockatoos,
and minute finches and wrens –
feathered perfections already
a fading future.

Possum, bandicoot and wallaby carcasses
line the road around the base:
victims of uncaring drivers;
or lie rotting in bushland
after being shot in sacrifice to
human perceived need or greed
and failure to understand
how we are all integral
for our mutual survival.
Already nostalgia seeps through my psyche;
I feel my spirit drowning in its incoming tide.
I cannot hide my pain
as I sense the tranquillity of a peaceful past
being hurled to extinction.

Collateral Damage

Syria 2017

Collateral Damage:
aged five, not terrorist
but terrified;
alone on a chair in a hospital hall
hair matted under
a cap of blood.

Collateral Damage:
five months old, dust covered
but recovered
rushed to hospital by her saviour;
together buried
beneath the bombed building.

Government and allies
rain death from
air-conditioned cockpits;
while citizens starve and die
and innocents pay the cost
for all that is lost.

The Game

It took only a picture:
a small girl screaming
stripped bare
by allies' flames
fleeing the ashes
of her shattered life.
That image
haunted newspapers
magazines
and blasted reality
from our television screens.
It propelled people
to think
to see
to protest for truth;
forced politicians
to listen
to act
to withdraw
propaganda
of what the war was for.
That land became one;
falling dominoes
did not come.

Yet still
flags are waved
more dollars
for weapons given
our armies driven
to the tune
of touted justice
on foreign fronts;
a former friend
deemed foe;
we set one
against the other
for what is declared
as right.
Western ways
infiltrate distant zones
tune out the moans
as graphic images
of innocents dying
pepper our minds
too many times.

Unconsumed food
is casually tossed
into bins
as visions of
balloon-bellied babies
and fretted torsos
loom on screens
in lounge rooms.
If we gaze too long
we might go insane
so we give our children
screened war games
numbing reality in
response to hard sell
of thrill and kill
and reincarnation
thus no death smell.

Our children are
sent to camps
for expensive adventure
while millions scratch
and beg to live
in camps of another kind
confined by need
to withdraw from home
and the violence caused
by arms-selling companies'
insatiable greed
and our misguided need.

For many
escape from conflict
brings hope
which we splatter
against our rocks of fear:
no refuge here.
Incarcerated children
given sentences
longer than
rapists or robbers;
offers of reprieve
fall on deaf ears.

Colonisation formed
the basis of our game
our pride
and our gain.
Today's smallest victims
with running noses
and fly pestered faces:
stark traces
of earliest memory
of our own beginning
winning a new nation
through another's dying
at our request.

Pictures of poverty
blind the beauty
of rich lives lived
in dignity
knowledge
and respect
before our European
ancestors came.
We call it progress;
some call it shame.

Now no lands remain
for us to attain
rule and assimilate
to self-perceived
superior ways.
So we declare war
against those
who threaten
or hold the means
to satisfy
our modern needs.

We blithely support
the like-minded
for greed or glory
under the rule
of the great one:
Injustice is his name
and it is he
who drives our ambition
to maintain our fame
no matter where
or how we play
the conqueror's game.

Jellyfish Dreams…

Jellyfish Dreams

She dreams of jellyfish:
  not the glutinous globes
      drying to death
            along the receding waterline.
Her jellyfish
  bloom and contract
            in an Attenborough blue sea
      shapes crystalline and translucent
      tentacled or frilled in fibrous lace
  darting and dancing
            in time to ocean's rhythm
  pulsating forms
      opaquely obscuring
      the centre of intelligence
            enabling their eons of existence.
She dreams of jellyfish:
  she, whose own reality
      is consciously concealed
            beyond a glazed shield.

Painted Desert 1976

Her rattle awakens dreams
as ancient as the land.
Onyx eyes gleam an invitation
to dare – to wholly share the moment
amid purple brushed rocks
and table top hills.
My mind stills.
I feel the bond of seeking solitude
beneath the petroglyph boulders
camouflaging our existence.

Each safe in her own space
we transcend time and place
until she gracefully uncoils
slowly she slithers
shimmering in the midday sun
until becoming one
with the desert sands.
Alone I stand, knowing
she takes with her
a part of my healing heart…

        I begin to understand.

Mountain Reflections

Early morning sun
splatters
with dappled swirls:
a vertical rocky portrayal
of Monet's nymphs
in lapis lazuli.

Midday's fiery orb
sharpens
definition of shape:
sky fades to backdrop
as mountain overwhelms
its dominions.

Evening's fading light
slices
its side with silver swords
sliding earthward
till lunar light reflects
a sleeping shadow.

Morning Ride Down Oxford Street

The last to board
she shook coins into the driver's palm
and turned
smack-ringed downcast eyes
briefly lifted
people shifted:
window preferences outweighed
by fear
Please God, don't let her sit here.
Blocked spaces, locked faces.

I guessed she was still in
her mid teens
her strappy dress and sandals
no protection
against the morning chill nor
I surmised
against ravages of the night before.
I slid aside
tapped the vacant seat and received
rasping *Thanks*.

She was pretty or would have been
had the city
not tossed her into its bin of
wasted existence.
I queried in voice consciously casual
You okay?
Hesitation from sagging head then
muffled *Yeah*
followed by a furtive look my way
Thank you.
Another glance caught my smile;
it was returned with a slow nod.
Short silence
Can I take you somewhere?
No, eyes drooped,
but wake me when we get to the Square…
going home.
I was certain the reply was a lie:
the Square offering a short cut
to Kings Cross.

But I obeyed.
Her slow blinking eyes were grateful
as she shakily stood.
Sure you're okay?
I handed her the fallen purse.
Yeah, she clasped the rail.
On the step she paused
stretched tall
Yeah, she beamed.
I'm okay…thanks.

My gaze followed her;
I acknowledged the wave
as she waited at the lights.
They changed;
the bus jolted towards the city centre.
Glancing back
I watched helplessly as towards the Cross
she went;
on board I heard only a muttered symphony
of contempt.

City Lunch Break

i

With my friend Agnes,
I headed across the intersection
of Hunter and Pitt,
attempting to walk away
the weariness of office;
we passed Australia Square,
its lofty tower high in the air.

We planned to purchase
sandwiches and fruit
at my favourite vegan place,
and return to the Square
to sit, chat and dine
with the people and pigeons
gathered there.

The slope of Hunter Street
decreased to half-width:
a cage protecting pedestrians
from a construction site;
with our high heels unclicking
on melting-hot pavement
we were jostled forwards.

A heel sank in dank bitumen
but my body rushed on,
being hopelessly propelled
by the lunchtime throng.
Helplessly I hobbled,
sadly wondering where
my shoe had gone.

When the street widened once more
a score of people paused,
formed a widening circle
of anticipation:
an audience to an unrehearsed play,
and for a brief moment,
I was a star that day.

A young man swept in front of me
dropped to his suit-clad bended knee;
in his right hand which he held aloft
a stiletto of fine leather, black and soft.
I see, said he, you are the maid
whose foot fits this shoe
I hold displayed.

Stress fell from faces all around;
cheers and laughter became the
lunchtime sound.

With Cinderella again fully shod;
my noble prince smiled,
gave a wink and a nod,
laid a kiss upon my extended hand
and with a flourish he bowed
before disappearing into
the clapping crowd.

With minds filled with wonder and elation,
in even-footed steps, Agnes and I skipped
to our destination.

ii

The gloom of a week before
faded from that place,
though sadness lingered
in memory of
a troubled man's leap
from the highest tower floor;
his despair and body smashing onto
the canvas canopy of a delivery van.
That tragic day we ran
back to our workplace security,
our faces as ashen as those who saw
from the windows of our thirteenth floor
the smashing glass, the body drop
to his final resting spot
where Agnes and I had passed
only moments before.

I remember...

for Leny

I remember
a bush cabin – unkempt, basic.
We filled it with laughter
and boys;
no toys. We two mums
led the way
each day
to a dam dug deep
in the forest –
succour for thirsty
unconcerned wombats
and skittish wallabies.

No light
at night we shone dull torches
flickered them into trees
startling possums
whose gleaming glares
brought grins of wonder
to youthful faces.

We fed
on home-baked bread
made to your Dutch recipe
served with vegetables
sown and grown with love
in the soil of our shared land.

I hold a photo
in my hand:

two women, young,
one tall, Aryan blonde,
one small and tanned.

Matching children –
two from you
and my one
shining under the
southern sun
on a week to remember –
carefree and fun.

Solace

Trees whisper welcome
fronded fingers beckon
and my heart heals
to the sound of trilling sonatas.
Even shrill shrieking songsters
splaying the mountain stillness
bring my mind peace.
A slither or creeping
creates a weaving distortion –
a disruption to the pattern of waving grass
discreetly breaking its rhythmic dance
in the beguiling summer breeze:
I am not alone.
But all that is here is Nature
and my heart and mind
succumb to her embrace.
I rest   I stay
blessed and refreshed by the truth
that such moments reveal:
I am nature too
and here I belong.

Maternal heritage

On Tasmanian spring evenings
we stood, arched bodied,
eyes achingly focussed
in frantic attempts to unscramble
the patterns her fingers traced
across the fathomless
spangled black blanket above.
Words like the pot, pointers,
copper kettle and Southern Cross
baffled my youthful brain
while marvelling at the myriads
mysteriously hanging there
dripping fantasy
and fuelling imagination.
In reverence and awe
we inherited the lore
of the Milky Way.

I have learned to see
through my mother's eyes
the constellations
as taught to her
by her mother, and so on
back through generations.
But I was to discover
through seeking for myself
the mischievous nature
of the shimmering
sacred seven sisters,
afraid always to blink
lest they become lost.

Their soporific soothing smudge
sprinkles blissful memories:
the Milky Way and the daughters of Atlas
lead this woman home.

Dark Journeys 1942

She rode a bicycle
to work:
early start, late finish.
On rain lashed days
her hooded-caped form
forded unavoidable pools;
mud daubs decorated
her sturdy shoes.
On winter white mornings
the wheels crackled
through frost
cloaking the road's rocks.
Her stockinged legs numb,
her cheeks frozen,
she pedalled
with patriotic determination.
Dawn's filtered light
flickered through trees
bordering cow meadows on her left;
bushes muffled the river to her right.

Night time returns
were guided
by a torch trussed
to handlebars –
only managers drove cars.
Workers and they
departed before dusk.
Desks tidied, power off,
her final daily task:
to secure the doors.
Alone she then
pushed two miles
through threatening gloom
along the track
from flax mill to town;
eyes and light
focussed defensively down;
ears alert for the sound
of enemy planes slicing
peace and the stars.

Shards

First perceived patterns
formed on timber floor:
a mirror shattered by
a two-year-old.
Distressed grandmother's
shrillness cracked that
silent hanging moment.
Words, indecipherable
to my juvenile ear,
except for *seven years*
as her tears dropped
onto the shards.
Scared-eyed
she patted my head,
shaking hers.
Seven years
again and again
she said.
Bad luck was recalled
when I heard the words
long after the period
of the curse had passed.

Gems of Guilt

The gems of guilt
  he gave
        she wore
circling her throat
  their sheen softening
        suppressed emotion;
or pinned against clothes
  they shone in defence
        of her damaged heart;
or hiding under gloves
  they glistened like tears
        on her unheld hands.

His token for sixty years
  of perceived forgiveness
        for macho meandering:
a golden brooch with
  diamonds and amethysts
        forming an exquisite flower;
never understanding that all
  she ever desired
        was his loyalty and love.

In old age he sat by her bed
   cradling his head
         muttering to himself
and to his constant companions
   Remorse and Self-pity
         who taunted him
and haunted his nights
   with visions of the riches
         he could have had.

In death she defiantly wore
         his final gift.

Sorted possessions produced
   only her selections
         of costume jewellery.
Gone were the gifted gems;
   in their stead for each child
         a generous cash bequest
given with her bounty of love.
   To him, only confusion at this:
         her one act of rebellion.

Ancestral Habits

Survivors of the war years didn't throw away a thing:
cardboard, paper, buttons, and tiny bits of string
were clipped, stacked, basketed, or tied in one big ball,
placed on shelves or in cupboards or hung on a wall.
Bottles, jars and boxes adorned any vacant space:
'a place for everything and everything in its place'
was the motto of my mother, thrifty, sweet and neat,
whose spotless white lawn dusters were cut from old bed sheets.
Her lunches were legendary among her kith and kin –
leftovers turned to tasty treats, to waste would be a sin.
Garbage was wrapped in paper packs, tied with wool or twine;
composting, recycling and rubbish reduction made her
a lady ahead of her time.

My father on the other hand hoarded rather than reuse;
to fetch a tool from his huge shed was a task we'd all refuse
for the building housed strange items, some oily, some
    growing fur;
there were pellets and powders in unlabelled bins, and paint
    too thick to stir.
There was sump oil, grease and mower fuel, and baits for all
    kinds of beasts,
cracked panes, vacuum cleaners, gramophones, blankets and
    woollen fleece.
Nails and tacks and hinges spilled from jars upon the shelves,
while cobwebs in great abundance were a law unto themselves –
they wrapped around the light bulbs, they clung onto the vice,
they decorated garden netting which housed a family of mice.
Not a man for organisation, Dad's domain was in disarray:
a gigantic cleaning job we reluctantly inherited
when he finally passed away.

Backyard Adventures

Before lawns became
pristine and pretentious,
perfect green carpets
prised free of weeds,
the back yard encouraged
childhood imagination.

Wet weekends were
mud-pie-making frenzies
challenging consistency of each
chocolate-coloured creation
to stand alone
decorated with wild growing
daisies and dandelions
and served on plastic platters.

Chickens chuckled in a pen
of palatial grandeur:
royals in the castle tower
oblivious to their fate.
Canaries whistled and twittered
in an enclosure against the wall
between the woodshed and laundry,
taunting the regular mewing
sentinels who sat casting spells
of potential escape into
ready claws and drooling jaws.

After school, the awaiting
of a parent's arrival
on dry days offered
foreign legion forays into
dry-grassed and barren soil
deserts of fantasy;
transposed on rain-filled days
to the tropical forest habitat
of a small-girl Tarzan –
lush grass mushed underfoot
as gumboots scattered
ferocious lions who watched
the evil-eyed eagles within
the wall-mounted eyrie;
vultures lurked in anticipation
of impending disaster
behind their wire barricades;
puddles became bottomless lakes
to be cautiously forded
lest misstepping and falling
onto the crocodiles
sure to be skulking therein.

The click of the front gate
marked adventure's end.
The heroine scurried from the scene:
a slightly soiled child
now seated on the back porch bench
where she had been told to wait –
shyly innocent and sedate.

We stayed and we played…

Just you and me in
morning's early hours
unfazed and alone
one in flowing frills,
   one adorned in flowers.

We harmonised words
of peace, love and dreams;
shared secrets in song
voiced various means of
   wild escape schemes.

Round camp fires we joined
with like-minded friends
chanting and strumming
for world conflicts and
   hatred to end.

We travelled the land
in rattling old cars
I drove while you sat
in sunshine by day, by night
   under the stars.

Drifting days now gone
still together we age
bound by the dreams
in songs we once shared
   on life's special stage.

And some days I am drawn
to your special place;
I hold and caress you;
the sound of your strings brings
   a smile to my face.

The Wild Duck

She seeks the solace of my sad breast
and shares some pain with me;
I stroke her head, her eyes attest
her need to be set free.
I hold her tight and wish her luck,
my tears I have to fight
as I finally release the sweet wild duck
into her world of flight.

Letting Go

Looking back is a strange place,
a potholed track leading
over mountains, through quicksand,
across valleys of flowers and thorns

torn or mended by nostalgia's
needles of forgetfulness.
Memory forgives or reviles,
draws smiles or tears.

Fears can taunt though bred
in the soil of long ago,
stalling a chance, impeding
the speed of success;

distress and frustration hold court
over positive thought or will,
but acceptance can germinate,
in fertile creativity, a seedling

needing to blossom into vibrancy
overpowering the past
as it borders the smooth path
of an unencumbered life.

Mother's Day

It arrives each year in its plastic wrap:
she holds it in her hand,
reads the predictive annual lines
wishing he could understand
that a little time taken from his busy life
to her would mean much more;
she does not desire an expensive gift,
and he lives on a distant shore
so that to see him on her special day
is way beyond her dream
yet she longs to decipher his untidy scrawl
amidst flowers, birds or a scenic stream;
to know he had made a special trip,
chosen one just right for her,
adding heartfelt words of life and love –
yes, that she would prefer.
She thinks of the times she has searched
vast shelves in various stores;
the satisfied sigh when she finally finds
an exact one to suit the cause.
Sadly she reads the words again:
short, succinct, emotionally deplete;
how she longs to hold a handwritten card…
with a sigh she presses delete.

Tapping

Tap, tap, tap…
her mother had tapped too
at work and at play
with fingers and shoe.

Her tapping had a strong beat:
six-eight time for letters,
two-four, a balance sheet.

At the end of each set of rhythmic bars
the carriage whizzed back
like a comet through stars.

At night her feet tapped upon the stage
as she danced and sang
popular songs of that age.

The funds that were raised by her group
supported the efforts
of their overseas troops.

Now her daughter, too, taps during the day
her eyes on a screen
and no rhythm at play.

At night she also has a dancing role
contorting her body
around a steel pole

while men at the bar ogle and leer
she gathers their cash
knowing next year

it will be she who flies away to explore
a world far away
from that seedy dance floor.

Her tapping is softer than her mum's ever was;
her ambition is greater
for a less noble cause.

Closing Doors at Christmas

The bar door slammed behind him;
   he tumbled onto the street.
The tolling of a bell aroused him;
   he stumbled to his feet.

Memory led him by the hand
   to a small side-chapel door.
He fearfully lurched into the church;
   a defenceless child once more.

He dropped hard onto a wooden pew
   and fumbled with the words
of hymns and prayers vaguely recalled;
   his mumbled efforts hardly heard.

His eyes raised in terror towards the priest
   but this one was dark and young.
The middle-aged man shook off the fog
   as a familiar song was sung.

He thought of the good life lost to drink:
   loving wife, three children, good pay.
He felt himself drowning in a sea of remorse,
   fell to his knees to tearfully pray.

His eyes then met those of an altar boy
   who gazed at him in sorrow;
there was something familiar about the lad –
   he would try to recall what tomorrow.

A tear trickled down his furrowed face
   as the service stirred something within.
The boy faded away as the man realised
   it was not he who was guilty of sin.

At the new dawn of day he felt finally free
   from an anger he had held within;
and he remembered the lad he had seen at Mass –
   the innocent boy he knew now had been him.

At Christmas next year he came back again
   to where the boy's sorrow and pain began;
gone were his demons, he now stood proud:
   a hurt boy had become a healed man.

The Dandelion

Dressed in
golden arrogance
the dandelion
waltzes with
whichever breeze
blows her way,
swaying alone amid
a ballroom of
formally clad
cultured companions,
she moves to
her own rhythm,
head held high;
other blooms
will soon
fade to blandness
while she will
transform to her
gentle grey phase
robed in a
feather-soft cloak,
standing erect and strong
as she counts the hours
till Death's kiss
disperses her seeds
to immortality.

Wandering Down Memory Lanes

They ooze away
        from the mainstream
  where dollars escape
  in the arms of desire;
  where a label
  can loosen logic;
  where coffee is served
  with elevated costs;
  where glazed façades
  tempt and tease,
  competing with those
  across a cold pavement.

These offshoots
        drift into darkness
where drooping globes
wink welcome;
where lead light panes
sparkle amid cobwebs;
where memorabilia
meld with smiles;
where once-loved clothes
come to life again
in the dreams
and warmth of memory.

Here there will be no
        pristine paperbacks
        packed with precision
        on soulless shelves;
    there will be no
        scented oils
        pumped into nostrils
        as feet cross portals;
    there will be no
        painted on smiles
        tracing steps to
        hard-sell wares;
    there will be no
        glances sliding down noses
        at touch of designer goods
        locked to security tags.

Here there will be
> a tinkling bell to
> bid you enter
> a special domain;
there will be
> tattered tomes and
> un-harried rummaging
> for treasured tales;
there will be
> the musty odour and
> muted dated décor
> of times long past;
there will be
> kind kindred spirits
> offering service and
> freedom to feel at home.

Keepsakes

Old books are classics *Old books fade and tatter*
old furniture antique *furniture needs constant care*
old wine rich and robust *old wine can be corked*
old cottages unique. *cottages descend to disrepair.*

Old wares are collectables *Old things can be broken*
old artworks great value *artworks hidden away*
old gardens are peaceful *old gardens become weedy*
old violins ring true. *violins too precious to play.*

Old religions mythological *Old religions can be rigid*
old happenings are history *events lose their impact*
old histories are legends *old legends unbelievable*
old folklore a mystery. *folk tales seem to lack fact.*

Old cars become vintage *Old cars can break down*
old standard's an old song *songs can be modernised*
old times are life's memories *old days soon seem quaint*
old monarchies hang on. *former dynasties ostracised.*

  Historical things may seem to last a long time
  when measured against the lifespan of mankind
  and though mortal minds gave these things birth
  changing trends alone establish their worth.

The Wreck

Turtle-like stranded
on its back
four wheels still
not struggling
like that creature's twitching limbs
grasping at the final
link to life.

The underside
untidy, unfinished
like the upturned shell
of Nature's housebound reptile,
accepting the onslaught
of ceaseless rain.

The solid upper armour
now below
has resisted the impact
shielding the unconnected
life within.

Not so, unfortunate turtle –
your protection is your tomb.

Roadkill

for Elisabeth

That sickening thud
  on a cold black night
meant death or maiming
  of a creature in flight;
neither we nor it
  had a chance to stop
in this tragedy of life –
  its final hop.

The verge too narrow
  to park upon,
no choice could we make
  but to keep driving on
with oncoming traffic
  and others behind;
we tried desperately
  to cast it from mind.

The sweeping vision
  of its floppy ears,
its pale coat and that sound
  brought silent tears;
in the early morning hours
  I lay wide awake
deciding on dawn's action
  I felt forced to take.

My car bumper bore
   strange evidence
adding more mystery
   to that sad event:
two small white marks
   where it had hit
but no signs of gore
   nor bloody bits.

I drove fearfully back
   to the accident site
where an innocent animal
   had died last night.
I gulped when I spotted
   a coat gleaming white
with splotches of red
   and no signs of life.

Its ears splayed flat out
   upon the ground;
it lay still and lifeless
   with not a sound.
I slowed and peered closer
   over the bank,
knowing that was our victim;
   I offered thanks,

with a smile on my face
   at the painted red art on
our hit and run critter:
   a large white carton.

The Ambulance Chaser

It only takes a siren
to raise his spirits high;
he will drop what he is doing
when the wailing fills the sky.
Never known for his agility,
he cannot move like he once did
but when a siren starts to scream
he can outrun any kid.
He scatters and he shatters
all things in his path;
he is alert and just as edgy
as a racehorse at the start.
He sprightly springs and lightly leaps
over chairs and through the house
like a kelpie over backs of sheep
or a scrawny scurrying mouse.
He fumbles and he bumbles,
keys clutched tightly in his hand;
runs across lawns to his front fence,
roars out his loud command:
'Which way was it heading –
was it west or to the east?'
his barking voice resounding
like a bloodhound tracking beasts.

As the shrieking vehicle veers
around the streets of town,
he reverses out his driveway
to track his quarry down.
With a manic smile upon his face
as his car wheels squeal and dance
he feeds his strange addiction
to pursue that ambulance.

Seeds of Contentment

The small town was armed with one man of law
who must have wondered what he was there for.
Torres Street started at the ancient stone church,
piously hidden by a giant silver birch.

Elderly widows lived on the left going down;
they shared average age with most of the town.
Weatherboard houses lining the opposite side
were also safe havens for old folk to abide.

Molly was known as the Torres Street tartar;
husband, Tom, enjoyed fame as the eternal martyr.
Their home stood severely two up from the end
with rarely a visit from family or friend.

Molly spoke loudly in a voice harsh and hard;
Tom whistled daily as he toiled in their yard.
Plants that he grew were the pride of his life,
being succulent sweet antitheses of his wife.

Neighbours shunned Molly for she always complained;
though from Tom's fruitful labours their larders gained,
till that sad barren summer of seventy-nine
and a new breed of tomato bore no fruit on its vine.

The bushes themselves were sturdy and tall,
filling all the spare spaces along the shed wall.
Tom composted, nurtured and frequently fertilised;
he'd not grown bushes like these, so hugely sized.

They had blossomed on time, with a strange kind of show;
but the chap at the pub said a bumper crop they would grow.
Yet, in the dry summer heat they began to wither and die;
Tom ripped them out by the roots and piled a stack high.

On a calm balmy morning Molly watched him set fire,
scoffed at his efforts to light the green funeral pyre.
Then with a swoosh the flickering flames took,
causing all in the vicinity to come take a look.

The flare from the fire attracted the brigade;
to the policeman's domain a phone call was made.
The ageing Vicar Vincento raced up Torres Street;
more folk followed the sweet smelling smoke from the heat.

Molly and Tom fought with a garden hose each
but rubber-like arms flopped unable to lift or to reach.
Sergeant Smith was alarmed to discover them there
snuggled up together like a pair of mating hare.

Then one of the widows gave a leap and a prance,
grabbed her sister's arm and they whirled in a dance.
The vicar's soft cackle became a raucous guffaw;
the brigade men were astounded by the sights that they saw

until they and the policeman joined together in mirth –
many lasting friendships that day were given birth.
The smoke churned and swirled well into the night
and folk fondly recall that time of special delight.

Next morning beamed brightly in a new warming glow;
on Molly's thin lips a welcoming smile seemed to grow.
The volume of Tom's whistle was heard three doors down
and a feeling of peace engulfed all of the town.

No charges were laid for they scarcely could be
as so many had joined in the accidental frivolity.
And Tom has a secret, he told me with a wink:
he has more seeds sprouting beneath his shed sink.

He's keeping them there to ensure life's always as sweet
as that time they got high in old Torres Street.

Dangers of Poetry

Poetry burns the biscuits
it boils potatoes dry
it snatches away the hours
making entire days fly by.
Poetry leaves beds unmade
and cultivates the weeds
it nags and niggles deep inside
planting impatient seeds.
Poetry strays eyes from focus
forcing them to stare into space
until the smell of scorching cloth
lifts the iron from that one place.
Poetry forgets to feed the dog
leaves the eggs beneath the chooks
it can move loved ones to act strange
and draws some doubtful looks.
Poetry forgets the calendar
erases important dates
it brings panic to many occasions
makes being late a regular state.
Poetry disturbs sleep at night
propels thoughts till early morn
such words from an exhausted brain
sometimes tossed away in scorn.

It is also a thing of wonder
how poetry can drive the car
for arrivals can be quite a surprise
did a poem take me so far?
Poetry is a cunning companion
yet it is always one I choose
to wile away the hours with
and one I would hate to lose.

The Art of Words

The breeze may be gentle
carrying words as soft as webs
to brush around the brain,
to skim across the psyche;
like fluttering feathers
they tickle and tantalise,
awakening thoughts to
a profound awareness of
some original concept of
beauty.

The wind may blow persistently
carrying words like tribal drums
to thrum across the mind,
to softly pound sorrow
or rap to rapturous heights;
beating out deep-held passions
or tapping the gamut of humanity's
emotions: its ugliness and its
beauty.

The shrieking gale lashes
gouging words from the skull
like a sharp-beaked predator
to hurl them against
complacency and ignorance.
Ghoulish syllables
stretch mental sinews upon
racks of ego and greed.
Yet in art, all words waft on winds of
beauty.

Stampede

A spark disturbs the leaf litter
   of a dawning brain;
it smoulders and smokes
   the semi-consciousness;
ignites imagination with
   increasing intensity
setting to furious flight
   a surge of words
disorganised and entangled like
   panicking beasts
following instinct to chaos
   in fleeing a wild forest fire.

From the crackling canopy
   they dash and dart
in haphazard unpredictability
   racing and spacing
from crowded crush
   to dispersed individuals:
a continuum of confusion
   unified in urgency;
the fierce and the meek
   gallop, stagger, scurry
in a unit of desperation
   all seeking safe destination.

The law of natural selection
   decides death or survival.
Exhausted, the fittest only
   finally fall in repose on the page.

www.ingramcontent.com/pod-product-compliance
Lightning Source LLC
Chambersburg PA
CBHW070938080526
44589CB00013B/1554